measuring sizes

An Aladdin Book
© Aladdin Books Ltd 1998
Produced by
Aladdin Books Ltd
28 Percy Street
London W1P 0LD

First published in Great Britain
in 1998 by
Aladdin Books/Watts Books
96 Leonard Street
London EC2A 4RH

ISBN 0-7496-3176-7

Project Editor: Sally Hewitt

Editor: Liz White

Design

David West • CHILDREN'S BOOK DESIGN

Designer: Simon Morse

Photography: Roger Vlitos

Illustrator: Tony Kenyon

Printed in Belgium

The author, Andrew King, is an experienced teacher.
He currently works for the London Borough of Richmond
as an advisory teacher for mathematics. He works with
children and runs courses for teachers.

The project editor, Sally Hewitt, is
an experienced teacher. She
writes and edits books for
children on a wide variety of
subjects including science, music
and maths.

MATHS *for fun*

measuring sizes

Andrew King

Aladdin / Watts

London • Sydney

CONTENTS

INTRODUCTION

Everywhere you look you will see lines, curves and shapes of different lengths and sizes. But do you know how to measure them? Make a racecourse, construct your own skeleton and have fun learning how to measure length, area, perimeter, volume and capacity.

Try the exciting activities, practical projects and fun games in this book, and you can learn about measuring sizes.

● Follow the STEP-BY-STEP INSTRUCTIONS to help you with the activities.

● Use the HELPFUL HINTS for clues about the experiments and games.

● Look at FURTHER IDEAS for information about other projects.

1 Yellow squares mean this is an easy activity.

2 Blue squares mean this is a medium level activity.

3 Pink squares mean this is a more difficult activity. You'll have to think hard!

LENGTH OF A LINE

How tall are you? How high can you reach? To answer questions like these we need to measure length. People used to measure length by counting up the number of hand lengths... but everyone's hands are slightly different. Now most people use a **standard measurement** like metres to measure length.

MAKE A METRE DERBY
Can your horse be first past the winning post?

1 Find a sheet of card. Fold it in half lengthways and cut it along the fold. Do the same again with another piece of card and stick the four parts together to make one long strip.

2 Starting from the bottom of the card, use a ruler with centimetres to draw a straight line up the middle.

3 Mark in all the centimetre spaces on the line from one at the bottom to 100 centimetres, which makes one metre, at the top.

4 Now you can decorate it to look like a racecourse. Make a winning post from some card and stand it at one end. Cut out two cardboard shapes of horses and riders. Decorate them brightly.

HELPFUL HINTS

● To make a neat join, turn over the card. Place the strips right next to each other, but not overlapping, then carefully stick some tape over the join. Now turn it over... a perfect finish!

5 Cut out a rectangle of thick card for each horse to stand on. To make the horse stand up, attach it to the base with two pieces of plasticine.

FURTHER IDEAS

● You can make the game even more fun by making some danger cards!

● If somebody throws a 1 they must pick up a card. The message might say 'Horse frightened by mouse, miss a go,' or how about 'High fence, go back 10cm!'

6 Place your horses at the start and take turns to roll the die and move your horse forward. The first past the post wins!

MEASURING CURVES

The difficult thing with rulers is that they are always straight. Unfortunately, most of the world isn't. In fact, it is wonderful how wiggly and bendy the world is. Without bumps and curves the world would be a far less interesting place! So, how can you go about measuring them?

WIGGLY WORMS
How good are your friends at guessing the right length of straight lines? What about wiggly lines? Make some wiggly worms to find out!

1 Find some string or thick coloured cord and measure out some different lengths against a ruler. You could cut lengths of 10, 14, 20 and 25 centimetres.

2 Stick the lengths of string in a wiggly line on pieces of card. These will be your worms. Now draw around each worm on the cards and decorate each worm to look really slimy!

3 Write the length of each worm on the back of the cards so you don't forget.

4 Challenge your friends to guess the length of each worm. The person that makes the nearest guess is the winner!

HELPFUL HINTS

● If some of your friends find it hard to make a good guess you could show them how to use a 'rule of thumb' to help.

Strangely enough with this 'rule of thumb' you use your little finger! Most little fingers are about 1cm wide so you can use it to move along the back of the worm to estimate its length.

FURTHER IDEAS

● Why don't you try estimating the length of edges! If you have got some old vegetables cut them in half and draw round the edge on a piece of paper. Guess how long each edge is and write it down.

● You can find out how long the edge really is by using some string to match along the edge of the outline and mark off the length. Next, straighten the string and measure its length against a ruler and check to see how close you really were!

VITAL STATISTICS

'Haven't you grown!' Whenever you meet someone who hasn't seen you for ages it's usually the first thing they say. Sometimes people call measurements of the body the **vital statistics**, you need to know yours to find clothes that will fit and comfortable shoes.

SKELETONS

You can make a skeleton to show your vital statistics!

1 Find some card and cut it up into long strips.

2 Measure from the base of your neck to your hips with a tape measure. Tape some strips together to match the measurement. This will be the backbone, write this on the strip so you don't forget.

3 Now measure the width of your hips. Cut a strip to match and join it to the other strip with a butterfly pin. Put the pin through both pieces of paper and bend the arms back. Ask an adult to help you with this.

4 Measure other parts of your body and pin them all on to make your skeleton! How many parts can you include? What about your fingers and toes?

HELPFUL HINTS

● You could draw a stick figure first to show the parts of your body you are going to measure. As you measure each part write it down on the stick figure picture.

● You can then cut all the strips of card to the right length and join them together. You could make some strips thicker to make your skeleton more realistic.

● You can add a skull to your skeleton by measuring round your head with a tape measure, make a strip to match the length, loop it over and stick it together.

● Do the same again, measuring round your head from top to bottom. Loop the strip round and stick it to the first skull loop.

● Make a bright face from pieces of card and stick this onto the head with tape.

AREA

Have you ever had new tiles put into your bathroom or kitchen? We call the space you want to cover, the **area**. Often the tiles are square in shape and this is how the size of an area is measured in squares.

TILE FLIPPING

To win this game you need to capture the area covered by the tiles by flipping all the squares over to your colour.

1 Find two pieces of different coloured card the same size. Stick them together back to back, then draw out a square grid on the card with lines about 4cm apart. The squares will be your tiles.

2 Cut 16 tiles out and now you are ready to play the game.

3 Turn the tiles so that eight are showing red and eight are green. Arrange them in a square.

4 The first player is the green team. He rolls a die. If a 3 is rolled, then three cards are turned over from red to green.

5 Now it is the red player's turn. He has one throw and turns back the number of cards shown on the die from green to red.

6 The die is then passed back and the battle to win all sixteen squares continues until one of the players captures them all!

HELPFUL HINTS

● When you stick the card together make sure you cover the whole sheet with a thin layer of glue. If you don't, some of the tiles might fall apart when they are cut into squares.

FURTHER IDEAS

● To play Tile Flipping you arranged the 16 square tiles to make a bigger square shape. What other numbers of tiles can you find that can be arranged to make a square? You could try four tiles, but there are others too. These are special numbers that are called, would you believe it, square numbers!

MEASURING AREA

Like measuring length not everything in the world comes in straight lines or simple squares that are easy to count and measure. Most areas that need measuring come in all sorts of unusual shapes.

BIG FOOT?
What do you think covers the greatest area, your foot or your hand? Have a quick look at them, press one against the other.

1 Draw a grid of squares on a piece of paper with your ruler. Helpful Hints tells you how to do this if you are stuck.

2 Place one of your feet on the grid and get a friend to draw around it with a bright marker pen. Colour in the shape of the foot so you can see it clearly.

3 Do the same again on another grid with your hand.

4 To find the area of the foot count all the whole squares inside the print.

but not one like this.

5 Next count all the squares that are more than half covered by the print. You would count a square like this...

6 What is the total area covered by your foot? Now count the squares covered by your hand. Which is the largest?

HELPFUL HINTS

● To make the grid of squares, line your ruler up with the edge of the paper and draw a straight line. Move the ruler along the paper so that the edge is now resting on the line you have just drawn. Draw a new line and repeat this across the page. Do the same moving across the page in the other direction like this to make the squares.

FURTHER IDEAS

● Why don't you find out the area covered by your mum or dad's foot?

● Make a guess and then find out. But watch out, they may have smelly feet!

CALCULATING AREA

You can't always find the area of something by counting squares! Sometimes it is easier to calculate area by using multiplication tables. If you need to find the area of a rectangle all you need to do is multiply the length by the width. So, for a rectangle that has sides of 3cm and 4cm the area is 3cm x 4cm = 12 **square centimetres**!

AREA ARITHMETIC

To be good at this game your friends will need good estimation skills and a good memory for number facts.

1 Plan some rectangles on a piece of scrap paper.

2 The first one might be 2cm long and 5cm wide, so the area would be 2cm x 5cm = 10 square centimetres.

5cm

2cm

4cm

4cm

3 The second might be 4cm long and 4cm wide, so the area would be 4cm x 4cm = 16 square centimetres. It is easy to see if you mark off the squares.

4 Make about ten different rectangles, draw them carefully on card. Don't mark in the individual squares. Mark each rectangle with a letter. Write the answers on a piece of paper and hide it from your friend.

A = 2cm²

B = 20cm²

C = 10cm²

D = 30cm²

HELPFUL HINTS

● To make it easier for some of your friends to play you could draw a square centimetre on the corner of each card to help them with their estimates.

1 square centimetre ⟶

5 Now challenge your friends to estimate the area of each of the rectangles. The most accurate person is the winner!

FURTHER IDEAS

● Have you noticed that some rectangles look different but have the same area!

● A rectangle with sides of 3cm and 6cm and one with sides 9cm and 2cm long both have the same area because 3cm x 6cm = 18 square centimetres and 2cm x 9cm = 18 square centimetres.

● Make up a new quiz. This time make all the rectangles different shapes but the same area. Do you think your friends will notice your trick?

PERIMETER

The **perimeter** of a shape is the line that goes around its edge. It is quite easy to work out the perimeter of some shapes with straight edges. You can measure the length of each edge with a ruler then add up the lengths to find the total. The lengths of each side of this triangle are 3cm, 4cm and 5cm. The total length is 3cm + 4cm + 5cm = 12cm.

STRING SHAPES

This is a fun way of making lots of strange and unusual shapes that all have the same perimeter length.

1 Measure out a piece of string about one metre long. Join the ends of the string with a piece of sticky tape like this.

2 Find a large piece of paper and put the string on it. Now arrange the string to make an interesting shape. Make sure the string doesn't loop over itself.

3 Now draw close to the outside edge of the string lightly with a pencil. Take the string away and paint the area on the inside of the perimeter your favourite colour.

4 Now paint the outside a different colour. Wait until the paint dries and then go over the perimeter again with a thick black marker pen to make it stand out.

5 Try making a new shape with the same piece of string – something that looks completely different. The perimeter will still be the same!

6 Whatever shape you have made with the string the perimeter will always be a metre!

HELPFUL HINTS

● To make it easier to draw round the string on the paper without it moving, you could stick down parts of it with some plasticine.

FURTHER IDEAS

● Can you make all the letters of your name in turn with the metre-length piece of string as the perimeter?

● You could make each letter on a separate piece of paper then decorate them to make them look colourful.

AREA AND PERIMETER

The perimeter goes all the way round a shape. The inside of the shape is called the area. Some shapes have the same area but the length of the perimeter might be longer or shorter, it doesn't always stay the same.

SQUARE SHUFFLING
Can you shuffle eight squares to make the longest possible perimeter?

1 When you have made eight square cards try an arrangement. One side of each square must touch one side of at least one other square.

2 If you arranged the cards like this, the perimeter would be 14 sides long.

3 What is the longest perimeter you can make?

4 If you think you have found the longest perimeter try to find the shortest!

HELPFUL HINTS

● A quick way of making a square from a piece of card is to gently fold over one of the corners to touch the side edge and then make a mark where it meets. Then fold over the end to that mark and make a sharp crease like this. Cut along the crease and you have a square.

Cut along crease

MORE IDEAS

● You can make the longest perimeter in lots of different ways. Here is one way of doing it.

● Did you find any others? Can you see how arrangements of squares that give the longest perimeter are similar? They all spread out the squares so that as many edges as possible of each square are part of the perimeter.

● Now you know this rule, can you quickly find a shape with twelve squares with the longest perimeter possible? It should have a perimeter 26 sides long. What would be the longest perimeter you could make if you used 24 squares? How about 30 squares?

TO THE MAX

One problem mathematicians often face is how to get the **maximum** out of something. Knowing how to find the maximum amount of area when the perimeter has to stay the same is very useful for solving lots of practical problems.

THE FARMER'S FENCE

Can you help the farmer to fix his fences so that he can make as much space for his chickens as possible?

1 The poor farmer is not very well off and can only afford 16 panels of fencing. The fences will only join together in a straight line or at right angles.

2 The farmer decides to make a plan. You could use old burnt matches, **but make sure you ask an adult first.**

3 He started by laying out the fences like this. The area inside the perimeter of the fence is ten squares.

He has another go. This time the area is worse! Only nine squares.

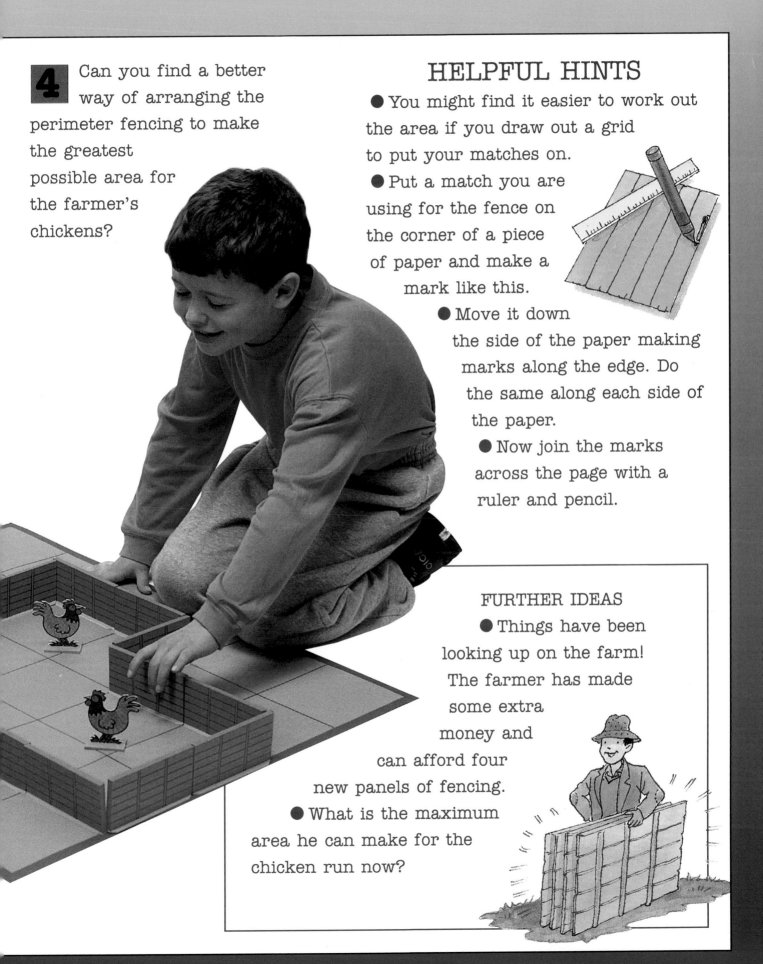

4 Can you find a better way of arranging the perimeter fencing to make the greatest possible area for the farmer's chickens?

HELPFUL HINTS

● You might find it easier to work out the area if you draw out a grid to put your matches on.

● Put a match you are using for the fence on the corner of a piece of paper and make a mark like this.

● Move it down the side of the paper making marks along the edge. Do the same along each side of the paper.

● Now join the marks across the page with a ruler and pencil.

FURTHER IDEAS

● Things have been looking up on the farm! The farmer has made some extra money and can afford four new panels of fencing.

● What is the maximum area he can make for the chicken run now?

VOLUME

You might have heard your mum or dad suggest that you 'turn the volume down and play quietly!' When mathematicians use the word **volume** they are not talking about the amount of sound that is made. The volume of a shape is the amount of space it takes up. It is often measured in centimetres cubed.

MAKIN' AND SHAPIN'
Can you shape a cube of play dough into amazing monsters?

1cm

1 First of all try making one **cubed centimetre**. Draw a square centimetre on a piece of paper as above.

2 Roll some play dough into a ball. Use two rulers to squash the sides until it fits the square. Keep doing this to all the sides until you have made a cube. You might have to add more dough or take some away to make each side of the cube fit the square.

3 Now you have made a cubed centimetre it doesn't matter what you do to it, squash it pinch it or push a hole through it – it will always be one cubed centimetre.

4 But one cubed centimetre is a little small. Draw out a square 5cm by 5cm. This makes an area of 5cm x 5cm = 25 square centimetres.

5 When you have made this larger cube it will be 5cm x 5cm x 5cm = 125 cubed centimetres. You can make some amazing monsters with a volume of this size!

FURTHER IDEAS

● It is amazing how large the volume of some small shapes can be.

● To find the volume of a cube you have to multiply the length of the edge by itself and then once more. So, the volume of a cube that has edges 2cm long would be 2cm x 2cm x 2cm = 8 cubed centimetres. What is the volume of a cube with edges of 10cm? What about 99cm? You may need a calculator to help.

CAPACITY

A ten-gallon hat was meant to have the **capacity** to hold ten gallons of water! Capacity is the way we measure the amount of substance a container will hold.

FILL IT UP!
How good are you at estimating the amount of water you need to fill up different containers?

1 Ask an adult if you can borrow some different empty containers like bottles and mugs from the kitchen. Now find an old bottle top and get a large jug of water.

2 How many full bottle tops of water do you think it will take to fill up the mug for example?

3 Write down all the different containers on a score card and make an estimate of the number of full bottle tops you think each one will hold.

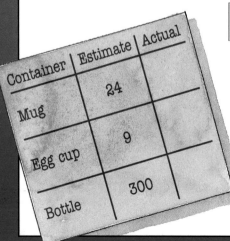

Container	Estimate	Actual
Mug	24	
Egg cup	9	
Bottle	300	

4 Now try filling the mug carefully. How many can it take before the water spills over the top? Write the total down on the score card. The person who makes the best estimate is the winner.

HELPFUL HINTS

● This can be quite a wet and messy game! It is a good idea to do the filling or pouring over a sink. If it is easier on a table put a towel down and place the containers on it to save everyone from getting a soaking!

FURTHER IDEAS

● Ask an adult if you can borrow a measuring jug from the kitchen.

● You can play a similar game with cups. This time fill a cup up to the brim and tip all the water into the jug. If you look on the side of the jug you can see the measuring marks. These might be in millilitres marked ml or fluid ounces, marked fl.oz. See if you can estimate how far up the measuring jug the water from a different size cup will go when you pour it in. How accurate can you make your estimates?

VOLUME OR CAPACITY?

Volume and capacity are similar. Volume is the amount of space occupied by an object and capacity refers to the amount of substance a container can hold. The capacity of a bottle holding 500ml does not change, but if you gulp some of the drink the volume of liquid is less.

WATER MUSIC
Some musical instruments make use of different volumes of air to make different notes. You can make your own bottle orchestra.

1 Ask an adult if you can borrow a glass bottle and a measuring jug. Tap the bottle with a pencil and listen to the sound it makes.

2 Try pouring in different volumes of water. Perhaps 50ml first.

3 Tap the outside of the bottle with a pencil. How has the sound changed? Yes! it is a higher note. Try 100ml, then 150ml. How is the sound affected now?

4 Try gathering some other glass bottles and make each have a different note. Can you make up a tune?

HELPFUL HINTS

● It is easier if you use bottles that are exactly the same. When you have found the amount of water in the bottle that gives you the note you want you can keep a record of what you have done by tipping all the water back into the measuring jug and noting down the amount.

● Have a look at the number of millilitres you used and write it down, so when you come to play your composition for bottles and orchestra you will know exactly how much to pour into each container!

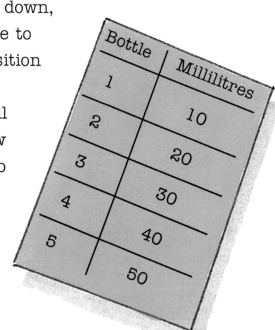

Bottle	Millilitres
1	
2	10
3	20
4	30
5	40
	50

COMMON MEASUREMENTS

AREA

 $= 1cm^2$

 $= 4cm^2$

$= 9cm^2$

$= 16cm^2$

LENGTH

10 millimetres = 1 centimetre

100 centimetre = 1 metre

1000 metres = 1 kilometre

VOLUME

 $= 8cm^3$ (cubed)

$27cm^3 =$ (cubed)

GLOSSARY

Area
The area is the size of a space inside a flat shape. We can measure area by counting the number of squares that cover a shape.

Capacity
Capacity is the way we measure the amount that something will hold. A jug that holds a litre of water has the capacity of one litre.

Cubed centimetres
A cubed centimetre is the volume of a cube measuring 1cm long, 1cm wide and 1cm high. One cubed centimetre is also written $1cm^3$.

Maximum
The maximum means the greatest or most. If you are working to the maximum it means you are working as hard as you possibly can.

Perimeter
The perimeter of a shape is the length of the line that goes all the way around its edge. You can add up the length of each side of a shape like a square to find out its perimeter. You can find out the perimeter of a shape with curved lines by measuring it with a piece of string.

Square centimetre
A square centimetre is the area of a square with sides of one centimetre long. Four square centimetres can be written $4cm^2$ and would fit into a square with sides of two centimetres long.

Standard measurements
The units of measurement we use, like centimetres, must always be the same or we cannot be sure how big anything is. Some standard units commonly used today are grams, millilitres and metres.

Vital statistics
Your vital statistics are all of your different measurements, like the size of your waist, the size of your shoes and how tall you are.

Volume
The volume of a shape is the amount of space it takes up. You would take up much less space than an elephant. Volume is usually measured in cubic centimetres.

INDEX